USBORNE SIMPLE READERS
THE BIG MATCH

Anne Civardi

Illustrated by Peter Wingham

Reading Consultant: Betty Root
Reading and Language Information Centre
Reading University, England.

This is Josh. He is mad about football.

He has a naughty little sister called Trixie.

And a twin sister called Jessie. Mungo, his dog, likes to play with his new football.

Dad, Mum and Jessie like playing football too.
Even Trixie knows how to play.

Josh is always practising new football tricks.
He makes everyone very cross.

Every morning, Josh exercises to keep fit.

Then he wakes up Trixie and Jessie.

They play football in the garden. Josh has to practise for the big match on Saturday.

After breakfast, Josh is going to train with his team.
He is the captain of the Strikers.

Mum takes him and the girls to the pitch.

Sid, the coach, is there waiting for him.

Sid talks to the Strikers about the big match.
They are going to play against the Hotshots.

Before they start training, the players run
around to warm up.

6

Sid teaches them how to tackle, dribble and kick the ball. And how to head it to each other.

The Strikers train hard for two hours and then have a rest. Now they are ready for the big match.

Mum comes to collect Josh, Jessie and Trixie. They say goodbye to their friends.

8

Dad has a surprise for Josh when he gets home.

He has bought Josh a new pair of football boots.

Josh gives his old ones to his sister, Jessie.

He wears his new boots everywhere, even in bed.

On the day of the match, Josh gets up early.
But he cannot find his new boots anywhere.

Trixie finds out that
Mungo is the thief.

10

She takes the boots
back to Josh.

Josh is so pleased he gives Trixie his scarf.

Then he gets ready for the big match.

It is almost time to leave. Everyone is going to watch Josh play.

Before the match starts, the Strikers warm up.
Sid gives them a few last-minute tips.

12

The Hotshots run on to the pitch. Josh thinks that they look like a very good team.

Josh shakes hands with their captain, Kev.

The referee tosses a coin before they begin.

Kev wins the toss and the Hotshots kick off.
They soon get the ball away from the Strikers.
14

Kev kicks it down to the end of the pitch. After only
five minutes, he scores the first goal.

15

The Hotshots are very proud of their captain.

Podge is unhappy. He let the ball into the goal.

The referee blows his whistle. Josh kicks off again and cheers on his team.

He passes the ball to Shortie who heads it to Bernie.
Bernie almost kicks it into the goal.

Now the Hotshots have the ball. Kev kicks it hard
but Podge makes a great save.

The players rest at half-time and eat oranges.
Josh talks to his team. He is sure they can win.

The game starts again.
The Hotshots attack.

Josh tackles Kev. Now
he has the ball.

He dribbles it down to the end of the pitch.

And with a big jump, heads it into the goal.

Josh bumps into the goalie and hurts his leg.

Podge and Shortie help him off the pitch.

Sid asks Jessie to play
instead of Josh.

She puts on shorts, a shirt
and some boots.

Then she runs on to the pitch, ready to play.
The Hotshots laugh when they see a girl coming.

Kev teases Jessie with the ball. He does not know how well she can play.

Jessie runs round Kev and gets the ball.

No one can stop her. She kicks it into the goal.

The referee blows his whistle and the big match is over. Jessie has helped the Strikers to win.

22

Sid, the coach, gives Jessie her own Strikers outfit.
Now she is one of the team.

Mum and Dad are proud of their twins. They are
the best footballers in the team.

Josh and Jessie are happy when they go to bed.
They are the champions of the big match.

First published in 1987. Usborne Publishing Ltd, 20 Garrick Street, London WC2E 9BJ, England. © Usborne Publishing Ltd, 1987